The Country Where Everyone's Name Is Fear

Країна, де ім'я кожного – страх

КРАЇНА, ДЕ ІМ'Я КОЖНОГО – СТРАХ

Вірші **Борис Херсонський** *і* **Людмила Херсонська**

Під редакцією **Кеті Фарріс** *та* **Іллі Камінського**

Переклали Кеті Фарріс, Ілля Камінський, Поліна Барскова, Алекс Сіґал, Владіслав Давідсон, Борис Дралюк, Ендрю Джанко, Остап Кінь, Ольга Лівшин, Ґрейс Магоні, Вальжина Морт, Євґеній Осташевський, Діана Сеусс, Кетерін Янг, та Хав'єр Замора

ВИДАВНИЦТВО ЛОСТ ГОРС

Ліберті Лейк, Вашингтон

THE COUNTRY WHERE EVERYONE'S NAME IS FEAR

Poems of Boris and Lyudmyla Khersonsky

Edited by Katie Farris and Ilya Kaminsky

Translated by Katie Farris and Ilya Kaminsky with Polina Barskova, Alex Cigale, Vladislav Davidzon, Boris Dralyuk, Andrew Janco, Ostap Kin, Olga Livshin, Grace Mahoney, Valzhyna Mort, Eugene Ostashevsky, Diane Seuss, Katherine E. Young, and Javier Zamora

LOST HORSE PRESS
Liberty Lake, Washington

ACKNOWLEDGMENTS

Some of the translations in this collection had previously appeared in *The Atlantic, The Nation, Modern Poetry in Translation, Tablet Magazine, Ploughshares, Poetry International, Tikkun, Tupelo Quarterly*. Several poems were anthologized in *Words for War*, ed. by Oksana Maksymchuk and Max Rosochinsky (Academic Studies Press, 2017).

Cover Image: *Raising the Banner* by Alexander Roitburd
Photo of Boris and Lyudmyla Khersonsky: Lesya Verba
Book Design: Christine Lysnewycz Holbert

Series Editor: Grace Mahoney

FIRST EDITION

This and other fine LOST HORSE PRESS titles may be viewed on our website at www.losthorsepress.org.

LIBRARY OF CONGRESS CATALOGING-IN-PUBLICATION DATA
Cataloging-in-Publication Data may be obtained from the Library of Congress.
ISBN 978-1-7364323-5-8

LOST HORSE PRESS
CONTEMPORARY UKRAINIAN
POETRY SERIES

Volume Nine

ЗМІСТ

CONTENTS

INTRODUCTION

On Boris and Lyudmyla Khersonsky

IN THE SUMMER OF 1992, the Soviet Union has just fallen apart. Three hours away from our apartment in Odesa, Ukraine, in the breakaway republic of Pridnesrovie, war has erupted. In six months, my family will leave the country, though we do not know it yet.

One morning, my father points to the door and gestures for me to open it, indicating that someone has knocked. On the other side is a tall and very beautiful woman who leans forward so I can read her lips and says in a language I had never seen, "I'm Lyudmyla, and I'm here to teach you English."

I won't meet Lyudmyla Khersonsky again for almost twenty years. In that time Ukraine will endure at least two revolutions, an invasion by the Russian Federation, and an ongoing war. Before we renew our long friendship, I will read many poems she writes witnessing the war, such as this piece:

> in a country where everyone's name is fear:
> it's good that you don't see a thing
> and don't hear a thing. Say to anyone not a thing.
> Slip nothing in your bra. Keep nothing
> in your pocket. In both ears, nothing. In two eyes, nothing.
> Blind feet. No looking back. No
> looking back. If you look back, my brave:
> if my brave, you look back, my brave: you say nothing
> when you arrive to a new destination
> they will learn nothing from you: they will learn what nothing is.

There is an unforgettable tone in her poems, one that clashes a chronicler's perspective, disgust with the state, and the intimacy of a witness, a whisperer of lines spoken with tenderness towards a human body caught in the wartime. The visceral, immediate, physical detail here serves both purposes:

> Buried in a human neck, a bullet looks like an eye, sewn in,
> an eye looking back at one's fate.

But in this war-time world, where the poet sees everything—
everything isn't always what it seems:

> See the tail that wags the dog.
> Language is speaking the man.
> Look, the shovel is making a hole in the grave digger!
> Brushes paint artists into the walls!
> The hip is wagging the dancer, see?
> That oar is rowing every person in the boat.
> Don't you see it? Here is a head that thinks a man into a man.

The question about the function of language in a time of crisis is especially urgent in Ukraine, where Putin's invasion began on the pretext of the protection of the sizable Russian-speaking population and their language. When the invasion began in 2014, I received the following e-mail:

> I am Boris Khersonsky and I work at Odesa National University where I have directed the department of Clinical Psychology since 1996. All that time I have been teaching in Russian, and no one has ever reprimanded me for 'ignoring' the official Ukrainian language of the state. I am more or less proficient in Ukrainian, but most of my students prefer lectures in Russian, and so I lecture in that language.
>
> I am a Russian language poet; my books have been published mostly in Moscow and St. Petersburg. My scholarly work has been published there as well. Never did anyone attack me for being a Russian poet and for teaching in the Russian language in Ukraine. Everywhere I read my poems in Russian and never did I encounter any complications. However, tomorrow I will read my lectures in the state language Ukrainian. This won't be merely a lecture—it will be a protest action in solidarity with the Ukrainian state. I call for my colleagues to join me in this action.

What does it mean for a poet to refuse to speak his own language? This uneasy relationship with speech is present everywhere in Boris's poems: "I can't open my mouth," he writes, "speech snaps like a wire / in the wind." A Soviet dissident, Boris Khersonsky's poems give us a historical panorama of Ukraine in the last century: revolution, world wars, the Holocaust, Soviet oppression. Here is a poem he wrote about a teacher of Ukrainian literature in Odesa, forcibly committed to a psychiatric hospital by Soviet authorities for encouraging students to learn about Holodomor, the Soviet-era man-made famine which the government maintained had never happened:

> They printed in the medical history:
> "There was no Holodomor.
> It was the stable delusion of Anna Mikhailenko,
> a teacher of Ukrainian literature."
> For seven years she was in a Special Psychiatric Hospital.
> It was a hybrid hospital—
> a madhouse and a prison.
> It was a time of hybrid hospitals. Now is time of a hybrid war.
> Seven years is a biblical phrase.
> "And Jacob served Laban seven years for Rachel.
> Because he loved her."
> Seven. Seven years.
> "Rachel calls for her children.
> She can't calm herself,
> Because they don't exist."

I first met Boris in the early 1990s when he edited the culture section at a local newspaper, *Odesskii Vestnik*. I was a deaf kid who knocked on his door with a bunch of poems, which he very kindly rejected. During my 2015 visit to Odesa, Boris and I agreed to meet at a neighborhood café in Odesa to chat about poetry. But when I arrived at the corner at 9:00 a.m., the sidewalk tables were overturned, rubble crowding the street from where the building had been bombed.

A police siren wailed through my fingertips. A crowd, including local media, gathered in the rubble around Boris as he spoke out against yet another fake humanitarian aid campaign of Putin's that precipitated the bombing. Some clapped; others shook their heads in disapproval.

A few months later, several explosives went off in Boris's apartment, breaking windows and leaving a hole in the floor. When Americans ask about that time in Ukraine, I think of the lines from Boris's poem:

> people carry explosives around the city
> In plastic shopping bags and little suitcases

•

Although they are married, and often write on similar themes, Boris and Lyudmyla's poetics are quite different. She primarily writes from the perspective and persona of direct witness, while his work gravitates more towards historical perspective and cultural context. Boris often writes longer sequences whose lushness of musical language and allusion have been compared to Joseph Brodsky's, while Lyudmyla's focus is on short lyrics with dramatic overtones. I can't help but be reminded of Anna Swir's work when I read her intimate, highly memorable lyric poems.

In preparing this collection, we did a brief interview with them—I include it here because it helps to highlight the way their voices emerge so differently from the same household:

Interviewer: In Lyudmyla's poems one hears the voices of people suffering as they experience war. In Boris's poems one hears the recollection of war. There is a kind of music of crisis in your work—

Boris: I will put it more crudely—not just the music of crisis, the muse of crisis, and even perhaps the muse of war.

Interviewer: What do you mean?

Boris: When gun machines aim at people, the muses aren't quiet; they scream.

Interviewer: how does that work in practice, on the page?

Boris: During the war, the texture of poetry separates into at least two paths: one is aphoristic, approaching things at a distance.

Interviewer: And another?

Boris: It's intimate, even lyrical.

Lyudmyla: Many literati want to act as if there is no war, no political crisis, or at least as if these aren't subjects worthy of poetry—they believe only the "immortal" subjects of poetry exist: motherhood, love, and so on.

Interviewer: And you?

Lyudmyla: And I would say that in a time of crisis, I want my poetry to amplify the voices of specific people—often those I have met. The philosophical perspective, the historical one? I leave that to Boris. In my work, I want real people.

Boris: Yes, I gravitate toward memory and philosophy, and the war has honed these aspects of my work. War has sharpened Lyudmyla's poems too, I feel.

Interviewer: Can you say more about this "sharpening"?

Boris: In war-time, everything is immediate. There is no speaking from a distance. Crisis and war sharpens our inner "I"—something fragile has been shattered into pieces, and the splinters cut as we write the poems, and cut into others as they read the poems.

Interviewer: And what of "immortal"?

Boris: Are these poems "immortal"? I hope they are not immortal. I hope war will become irrelevant.

Interviewer: How do two poets live under the same roof?

Lyudmyla: We respect each other's writing—it is that simple. We have similar viewpoints, but our poetics differ.

Boris: It is wonderful to be two poets who live under the same roof! We live in love and in agreement! As to writing—I get up at five in the morning. Lyudmyla goes to bed quite late. We divide the hours.

It's comforting for me to know that no matter the hour, a Khersonsky is keeping watch. I feel honored to help present these muses of crisis in English for the first time. Poetry is the better for it.

—Ilya Kaminsky

On This Translation

Writers do their thing, Saramago said, but without translators there is no world literature. We believe that great poetry should have many translators, so this short volume is a compendium of many, from different walks of life, with differing aesthetics, all performing the strangely intimate act of translation. Some translators herein are native Russian speakers and others live primarily in English; some are academics and others consider poetry their vocation, if not their job. To showcase the work of translation and show how every translator has a distinctive style just as every poet does, we have included two different translations of one poem each by Boris and Lyudmyla. We hope it shows the importance of multiple translations, which enrich English at large as well as expanding the poetic conversation past what any single translator, no matter how dynamic or talented, could manage.

For instance, here is Valzhyna Mort's translation of Lyudmyla Khersonsky:

> She dreamed a humanitarian convoy entered the city.
> Covered with a sheet head to toe, she sleeps, tucking her knees,
> always on her right side, while a wall watches her back,
> this is how one sleeps in the time of
> humanitarian wars.
> This is how in all times
> all tribes sleep,

waking only from silence, silence is a threat,
during silence, do not open
your door—
they are there, humanitarians with their inverted eyes.

And here is Katherine Young's translation of the same poem:

One night, a humanitarian convoy arrived in her dream.
Legs drawn to her chest, head under the sheet,
she sleeps on her right side, back braced by the wall,
the way people sleep during humanitarian wars.
The same exact way all tribes sleep at all times,
Waking only because of silence, that awful silence,
During that silence, don't open the gates—
Behind them, little humanitarians, heads facing the wrong way.

Comparing the two, an attentive reader will learn a great deal about
what is possible in English; this pairing is a masterclass in line-break,
word choice and syntax.

The reader might also be interested to compare two different
translations of Boris's poem "Explosions are the new normal." Here
is a translation by Polina Barskova and Ostap Kin:

explosions are the new normal, you grow used to them
stop noticing that you, with your ordinary ways, are a goner
a trigger man and a sapper wander around the park
whispering like a couple—I wish I could eavesdrop

surely, it goes this way: where there's a shovel, there's a tunnel
where there's a conspiracy, there's a catch
where there's God, there's a threshold
stalky Ukrainians—where granny tends to a garden patch

surely it's about the meaning of death, sudden as a mudslide
surely it's about the vodka: to relieve mortal anguish
once you've shown you have any brain, they'll brain you hard
    into submission
hair impeccably parted—where you spot a geometrically
    neat moustache

a trigger man and a sapper wander around like a couple
as the angel of destruction observes them tenderly from the cloud
we're captive birds dear brother that's it that's all
black sun of melancholy shines like a shrapnel hole

And here is a translation of the same poem done by Vladislav
Davidzon and Eugene Ostashevsky:

explosions norm of life coming to terms with them you
stop noticing man it be your end
the sapper and demolition man arm-in-arm in the park
whisper in each other's ear what are they saying

get the gist of the action shovel means undermine
conspiracy means undermine, underhanded means overkill
granny grew plain dill under the rain that fell mainly
elderly lady means elderberry, God means year

you get the gist of death out of the blue avalanche
gist of vodka for mortals to handle loss
mind means undermined means over and out
black square of a mustache means till death do we part

sapper and demolition pal arm-in-arm in the alley
terminating angel beholds them holds them with love
we are unfreebirds good night sweet prints turning read
shines the black sun the no one's rose of a shell shard

Translation should be similar but not very same to the original,
Petrarch once said. The similarity, he argued, should not be like that
of a painting or a statue to the person represented, but rather like
that of a son to a father, where there is a shadowy something—akin to
what painters call one's air—hovering about the face, and especially
in the eyes, out of which there grows a likeness.

Placed alongside each other, these versions give a fascinating lesson
on what English can do with diction and tone. There is also various
use of allusion, for instance the final line variously echoing Paul Celan.

Boris Khersonsky had studied Ukrainian in school but had published poems only in Russian until the language question in Ukraine became a question of war. At that point, he began to write poems in Ukrainian in solidarity with his county, and those poems have been published widely.

Lyudmyla Khersonsky was born in the republic of Moldova, and so Ukrainian wasn't a part of her formal education. Recently, she has written poems in Ukrainian while learning the language. This volume includes translations from both Ukrainian and Russian.

This book goes to print in the first days of the 2022 escalation of the war first waged by Russia in 2014. Ukrainian cities and villages have been bombarded by Russia, including homes and residences, schools, maternity wards, playgrounds, theaters and other cultural institutions, hospitals, and churches. There are now over three million refugees who have crossed the borders into Poland, Slovakia, Romania, and Moldova.

– Katie Farris

ЛЮДМИЛА ХЕРСОНЬСКА

LYUDMYLA KHERSONSKY

Ночью ей снилось, что ввели гуманитарный конвой.
Она спит, поджав ноги к животу, укрывшись простыней с головой,
на одном и том же правом боку, укрывшись стеной со спины,
так, как спят во времена гуманитарной войны.
Так, как спят во все времена все племена,
просыпаясь только от тишины, тишина страшна,
во время тишины нельзя открывать ворот —
за ними гуманитарные человечки с головою наоборот.

SHE DREAMED OF A HUMANITARIAN CONVOY

She dreamed a humanitarian convoy entered the city.
Covered with a sheet head to toe, she sleeps, tucking her knees,
always on her right side, while a wall watches her back,
this is how one sleeps in the time of
humanitarian wars.
This is how in all times
all tribes sleep,
waking only from silence, silence is a threat,
during silence, do not open
your door—
they are there, humanitarians with their inverted eyes.

Translated by Valzhyna Mort

Пуля в человеческой шее выглядит как вшитый глаз,
как будто человек смотрит глазом из затылка своей судьбы.
Кто стрелял в спину? Кто отдавал приказ?
Кто будет хоронить и почем гробы?
Все человеческое начинается и заканчивается войной.
Кто бы ни наступал, не поворачивайся спиной.
Говорит Господь: – Это от того, что народ Мой глуп, не знает Меня,
Неразумные они дети и нет смысла у них,
А дети думают, что они крепки, как броня,
что их массово шьют, и на всех хватит портних –
эти латают дыры, сшивают шейные позвонки,
пришивают оторванные пуговицы от руки.
А Господь говорит: – Они умны на зло,
но, – говорит Господь, – не умеют делать добра.
А неразумные дети, если выживут, думают, повезло,
А если умрут, думают, это было вчера,
а сегодня уже другой день,
и портнихи стоят с покрывалом и говорят: – Надень.
Долго ли видеть знамя, слушать звуки трубы?
Что за зверь пробудился? С кем воюет спецназ?
Кто стрелял в спину? Кто отдавал приказ?
Кто будет хоронить и почем гробы?

BURIED IN A HUMAN NECK, A BULLET

Buried in a human neck, a bullet looks like an eye, sewn in,
an eye looking back at one's fate.
Who shot him there? Who gave the order, which man?
Who will bury him, and what's the rate?
When it comes to humanity, war is the beginning and end.
Whoever attacks you, don't turn your back.
Says the Lord: For my people are foolish, they have not known me,
they are silly children and they have no understanding.
But the children feel as strong as their machinery,
mass-produced, with plenty of seamstresses for repairing:
some ladies patch holes, others fix neck bones,
still more sew on buttons that were torn away from hands.
And the Lord says: They are wise in doing evil—but,
says the Lord—they do not know how to do good.
But the children, if they survive, say it was luck,
and if they die, they think that was yesterday,
today is another day,
and the seamstresses stand with a shroud, telling them, "Put this on."
How long must we put up with the flags, the trumpets calling us
    into the fray?
What beast has awakened? Where did our special forces land?
Who shot that man in the back? Who gave the command?
Who will bury him, and what's the rate?

Translated by Olga Livshin and Andrew Janco

Страна как лужа лежит на военной карте,
на любую страну нападают в марте,
июне, июле, августе, сентябре, октябре,
пока дождь за окном и карты лежат во дворе.
Стой, кто идет, генерал на ватных ногах,
за ним человек без мира, а миру — швах,
миру шах и мат трехэтажный мат запрещен,
так и будет мир на грани войны пещер.
Чемодан, чистилище-ад, перед ним вокзал.
Кто сказал, что войны не будет? Никто не сказал.
Маленький серый человек
отменил двадцать первый век,
перевел стрелки страны
на зимнее время войны.

A COUNTRY IN THE SHAPE OF A PUDDLE

A country in the shape of a puddle, on the map.
Any country is an easy target in March,
in June, July, August, September, October,
as long as it rains
and maps litter the street.
Stop, who goes there, General Oaken Knees.
Red Square of his naked chest shines the way.
And behind him, a half-shadow, half-man,
half-orphan, half-exile, whose mouth is as coarse
as his land—
double-land where every cave is at war.
Do you say there won't be a war? I say nothing.
A small gray person cancels
this twenty first century,
adjusts his country's clocks
for the winter war.

Translated by Valzhyna Mort

Язык как зуб – коренной, молочный,
пальцем расшатать, привязать к двери, выдернуть...
В детстве вырастает другой,
в зрелом возрасте так и будешь ходить с дырой.
Можно, конечно, поставить имплант,
но, говорят, он не всегда приживается.
А тут еще эти фантомные боли –
вроде уже улыбаешься белозубой улыбкой,
а выдернутый продолжает болеть по-прежнему...

LANGUAGE IS LIKE A TOOTH

Language is like a tooth—a molar, a milk tooth—
that's loosened by a finger, strung to a door, ripped . . .
In childhood, another tooth grows.
But as an adult: you walk around with a hole.
You can, of course, get an implant,
but, they say, it won't make you whole.
And there's also these phantom pains—
you smile a white-toothed grin
but the one you pulled throbs the same. Lift up your chin.

Translated by Grace Mahoney

в стране, где все боятся,
ничего, что ты ничего не видишь,
ничего не слышишь, никому не скажешь
за пазуху не положишь, в кармане не держишь
в оба уха, в два глаза, в слепые ноги,
куда глаза не глядят, уходишь,
идешь, не оглядываешься, смелый,
ничего не слышишь, никому не скажешь
а куда придешь в новое место,
то и там ничего от тебя не узнают

IN A COUNTRY WHERE EVERYONE'S NAME IS FEAR

in a country where everyone's name is fear:
it's good that you don't see a thing
and don't hear a thing. Say to anyone not a thing.
Slip nothing in your bra. Keep nothing
in your pocket. In both ears, nothing. In two eyes, nothing.
Blind feet. No looking back. No
looking back. If you look back, my brave:
if my brave, you look back, my brave: you say nothing
when you arrive to a new destination
they will learn nothing from you: they will learn what nothing is.

Translated by Grace Mahoney

ЧТО ЕЩЕ МОЖНО СКАЗАТЬ О ЧЕЛОВЕКЕ КРОМЕ ТОГО, ЧТО ОН ОДИНОК?

Что еще такого, чего он сам бы сказать не мог?
Ни в сказке сказать, ни пером описать?
Чем еще в человека бросать?

Бросают в человека камни, бомбы, гранаты,
   а человек так же одинок, как когда-то,
умирает один, в одиночку хрипит.
Что еще можно о человеке, пока он спит?

Пока спит один или отвернулся к стене?
Один человек к стене, не нужный стране,
другой человек к стене, четыре стены,
один человек к стенке, эхо войны.

Ухо войны, один человек шумит,
как в раковине морской поселился кит,
как в клетке сердца один поселился страх. Один человек-прах
один человек от праха, бежит куда?
Глаза глядят. Человеку нужна еда,
кров над головой, солнце над головой, смех.
   Кровь над головой, один человек за всех.

Никто за одного. Хотя бы один? Никто. Человек в беде,
   в смерти, в бюро, в лито,
в офисе, в лифте, в подвале, в бою один.
Человек-брюнет, рыжий человек, блондин,
белый человек, черный человек, цветной, красный человек
   от горя с одной стеной.
Спит черствым калачиком, отвернулся к стене,
один в бесстыжей множественной войне.

HOW TO DESCRIBE

How to describe a human other than he's alone—
what to add?
(Pockets full of posies? A little lamb for Mary?)
What else is there to cast at a man?

A human is alone whether he dies or
snores. What else to say about a sleeping man?

Is a man sleeping or simply turned to a wall?
A man turned to a wall not to see his nation.

Another turned to a wall between four walls,
a man who turned to a wall, weary of war.
Ear of the war: so much noise from a single man,
as if a whale was birthed into a common shell,
as if fear was trapped in the heart's punchbag.
A lonely human is dust,
where to run from dust?
Where the nose points? But a person needs lunch.
A roof over his head, a sun over his head, and also to laugh.
Blood over his head, and also to bleed,
one man for all man.

No man for one man. Anybody? No one.

A man in trouble, in death, in office, in line,
in vogue, in disguise, in conflict: everywhere alone.
A brown-haired man, a redhead, a blond,
a white man, a black man, a rainbow-man,
one person: singled red with sorrow, by one wall.

Translated by Valzhyna Mort

На самом же деле, если укрыться одеялом вот так, с головой,
тогда сто процентов не будет второй мировой,
главное, лежать не дышать, не высовывать из-под одеяла ногу,
или высовывать, но понемногу.
Иногда можно вот так остановить войну —
осторожно высунуть ногу, потом еще одну,
потом повернуться на бок, лицом к стене,
спиной развернуться к войне —
пусть за спиной делает что попало,
нужно только зажмурить глаза, на голову натянуть одеяло,
запастись хлебом, и когда мир сторожить станет совсем невмочь,
отламывать его по кусочку и есть всю ночь.

HIDE UNDER THE BLANKET
AND PULL IT OVER YOUR HEAD

Did you know that if you hide under a blanket and pull it over your head,
then, for sure, World War II won't happen? Instead,
lay there don't breathe, don't let your feet stick out,
or, if you do, stick one out bit by bit.
Or try this helpful trick to stop a war:
first, carefully stick out one foot, then the other, now touch the floor,
lay back down, turn to one side, facing the wall,
turn your back to the war:
now that it's behind your back, it can thrash and shred,
you just close your eyes, pull the blanket over your head, stock up on bread,
and when you just can't deal with caring for peace anymore,
tear off some chunks, and when the night comes, eat what you've stored.

Translated by Olga Livshin and Andrew Janco

голосуем за вхождение страны в железнодорожный состав,
наш паровоз, локомотив истории,
железный утюг, однорукий бандит, военный устав,
танчики, танчики на чужой территории.
Танцы, танцы на дьду,
олимпийский факел каждому дому,
спасибо этому, переходим к другому,
на нашу голову, на чужую беду.

VOTE FOR OUR COUNTRY BECOMING A WAGON

We vote. Vote for our country. For our country becoming a wagon
    in the railroad transport
of history. Our engine, an old flatiron. Our one-armed bandit,
    an article of war.
Little tanks, little tanks creep. Into someone else's court,
dance. Our dancing the ice:
an Olympic torch in each kitchen. In each face: a stolen seaport.
Tanks aim at that port. On to the next. In short, we
are moving on to another port inside another. Tanks are hooting beliefs
into someone else's grief.

Translated by Grace Mahoney

вышел и споткнулся о людей,
близорукий, худой, мама говорила, птичий,
птичий очкарик с высоким клювом
споткнулся о людей-носорогов.
надо было уехать, не выходя из дому,
на цветной карандашный остров бурано,
с нарисованными домиком солнцем морем,
откуда очкарики поднимаются в небо
где на высоте птичьего полета
у очков запотевают счастливые стекла

WENT OUT AND STUMBLED OVER PEOPLE

Went out and stumbled over people.
Myopic, skinny mamma's boy,
a bespectacled bird with a high beak.
Walked out and tripped over rhino-people.
He had to leave without leaving the house,
to the sun-painted island of Burano.
To a house painted by the sun in the sea;
where sea paints us, us, bespectacled, as we rise
into the sky. From a bird's eye view
it is there—is it?—Happiness, fogging up our glasses

Translated by Katie Farris and Ilya Kaminsky

ЯБЛОКО

Ира Караимова умерла в первом классе.
На похороны назначили отличников – меня и Генку.
Мы никогда раньше не видели покойников.
Ира лежала в длинной белой шкатулке
в кружевах и в белых колготах.
На смуглом лбу – широкая белая лента.
Как будто ее ранили на войне в черно-белом кино.
Если бы она не умерла, ленту завязали бы бантом,– подумала я.
Взрослые шептались про то, что опухоль мозга и череп вскрывали.
Меня занимала атласная белая лента.
Вернее то, что под ней скрывали.
Ира лежала – большая смуглая кукла.
Взрослые шептались про то, как она вытянулась.
Ира всегда была высокой,– подумала я.
Мама Иры поцеловала меня и Генку солеными губами.
Спохватившись, дала нам большое яблоко.
Одно на двоих.
По дороге домой я все время думала,
как мы будем делить это яблоко.

APPLE

Ira Karaimova died in first grade.
The straight-A students were assigned
to her funeral. Perfect grades, just me and Genka.

We'd never seen a dead person before.
Ira, the dead girl, wore lace. A lace dress
within her jewelry box coffin. White tights.

Across her forehead, a wide white ribbon.
A ribbon, as if she'd been wounded in war.
A bandaged girl in a black-and-white war film.

Had she not died they would have tied
the ribbon in a bow. That was the thought I held
in my mind. I could hear the adults whisper.

They whispered of a brain tumor. That her skull
had been opened, like a chest full of treasure.
The ribbon. Satin. White. I was fascinated by it,

or by what hid beneath it. A toy that did not want
to be found. Ira lay there, a big doll. Sun-kissed.
The adults whispered. Whispered about Ira's body.

How she now appeared longer than before, almost
too long for her box. But Ira had always been tall.
A tall one, I thought. Ira's mother kissed me

and Genka with salty lips. Lips cold and white
with salt. Then, as if suddenly remembering,
she handed us a large apple. One apple

for the two of us. Me and Genka. Two.
How were we expected to share a single fruit?
A mystery I held all the way home.

Translated by Diane Seuss with Oksana Maksymchuk

УБОРКА

Каждый раз, когда он уезжает, она убирает в дому,
выбрасывает старые вещи, бумаги, книги.
Зачем, спрашивается, столько книг ему одному,
зачем ему атлас мира и путеводитель по Риге?
Каждый раз, когда он приезжает, чтоб ничего не найти,
он вверх дном перерывает дом.— Где моя черная папка?
Ты выбросила ее, выбросила?— Выбросила, прости.
У нее в голове веник, в руках — мокрая тряпка.

Она хлопочет на кухне, муж сидит на полу,
суп уже остывает, а муж не идет к столу,
ползает среди старых фото, выпавших из альбома —
вот девочка с мишкой, вот дедушка в кителе,
а где мои родители? Господи, где родители?
— Совсем сошел с ума. Твои родители умерли, Шлёма.

KEEPING HOUSE

Every time he leaves the house, she cleans.
Tosses out his old papers.
Why does he need all these
timeworn books? She drags out the sweeper,

whisks away the scraps. He's only one man,
and all this! Then, eureka—
under one pile, a sardine can.
A world atlas, and a guidebook for Riga.

He circles back home. Back
home? Everything is missing!
His papers, his books. His sack of maps.
Where's my black folder? He's fishing

for it. Did you throw away my black folder?
Yes. I'm sorry. It's gone.
Her broomstick in one hand. Wet rag in the other.
Her lips hold back a yawn.

He crawls through a spill of old photos on the floor.
Here, a small girl with a teddy bear.
There, a grandpa in uniform,
cap pushed down over his gray hair.

Where are my parents? Dear god,
my parents! You're going mad, she says.
Come to the table. Your soup is growing cold.
Get off the floor. Your parents are dead, Shlema.

Translated by Diane Seuss with Oksana Maksymchuk

хвост, который виляет собакой,
язык, разговаривающий человеком,
лопата, закапывающая гробокопателя,
кисть, рисующая художника,
бедро, виляющее танцовщицей,
весло, гребущее теми, кто в лодке,
голова, думающая человеком,
да мало ли...

SEE THE TAIL THAT WAGS THE DOG

See the tail that wags the dog.
Language is speaking the man.
Look, the shovel is making a hole in the grave digger!
Brushes paint artists into the walls!
The hip is wagging the dancer, see?
That oar is rowing every person in the boat.
Don't you see it? Here is a head that thinks a man into a man.

Translated by Katie Farris and Ilya Kaminsky

и вот, она уже знает, что делать.
нужно просто вселить человека в вирус,
желательно, молодую пару, чтобы они
занимались в вирусе сексом, размножались
до бесконечности, увеличивали потомство,
чтобы вирус заболел человеком, переносил
человека от вируса к вирусу, тогда
можно остановить пандемию

YES NOW SHE UNDERSTANDS IT ALL

Yes now she understands it all.
It is necessary to insert a homo sapiens into a virus.
Preferably two young homo sapiens that couple
endlessly, making little homo sapiens,
sexing sex in every endless sex.
So that virus becomes infected with homo sapiens, and passes
the infection along to the next virus and the next and the next—
That is how you stop a pandemic.

Translated by Katie Farris and Ilya Kaminsky

27

Ночью ей снилось, что ввели гуманитарный конвой.
Она спит, поджав ноги к животу, укрывшись простыней с головой,
на одном и том же правом боку, укрывшись стеной со спины,
так, как спят во времена гуманитарной войны.
Так, как спят во все времена все племена,
просыпаясь только от тишины, тишина страшна,
во время тишины нельзя открывать ворот —
за ними гуманитарные человечки с головою наоборот.

ONE NIGHT, A HUMANITARIAN CONVOY ARRIVED IN HER DREAM

One night, a humanitarian convoy arrived in her dream.
Legs drawn to her chest, head under the sheet,
she sleeps on her right side, back braced by the wall,
the way people sleep during humanitarian wars.
The same exact way all tribes sleep at all times,
Waking only because of silence, that awful silence,
During that silence, don't open the gates—
Behind them, little humanitarians, heads facing the wrong way.

Translated by Katherine E. Young

Дивіться на неї, вона втратила мову,
якою це все називається.
Без мови ніяк не назвати.
Хлопчик-каліка, не може ходити,
теж вчора мовчав – язик запав,
він бив себе по губах, хотів витягти звук,
але не вийшло, і встати не вийшло, і замахав рукою,
як він робив раніше, коли відвертався і прощався.

LOOK AT HER, SHE'S LOST HER TONGUE

Look at her, she's lost her tongue.
What is it all called?
How to name each thing without language?
And, look—the boy who can't walk,
he was also silent yesterday – his tongue sank,
and so he beat himself on the lips, trying to make a sound,
it did not work, and it did not work, and he waved his hand like
    he had done before,
and was spinning goodbye.

Translated by Katie Farris and Ilya Kaminsky

БОРИС ХЕРСОНСЬКИЙ

BORIS KHERSONSKY

страна приветствует оккупантов как говорится хлеб соль
овощные блюда кабачки томаты фасоль
ошметки плоти свиной центральный проспект длиной
в пять километров ведущий в обещанный мир иной
дети первыми учат слова на таинственном языке
говорят на чудовищной смеси родителям не понять
вышел приказ строить дома исключительно на песке
и строят все выше и выше взгляд не поднять
потому что верхушки зданий теряются в облаках
старцы мобилизованы и служат в небесных полках
в общем жизнь будет счастливой по крайней мере до той поры
пока оккупанты не провалятся в тартарары
пока военная техника не заржавеет на пустырях
пока не вымрут подростки с серьгами в ушах и ноздрях
родина мать виновата сама воспитала нерях
и стоит одна одинешенька до скончания дней
а буханка окаменела и пустая солонка на ней

THE NATION WELCOMES OCCUPANTS
WITH AS THEY SAY BREAD AND SALT

The nation welcomes occupants with as they say bread and salt
various vegetable dishes squashes beans tomatoes
scraps of pig flesh the central avenue five kilometers
long leads us into that other promised world
the children are first to learn the words of the mysterious language
speak an abominable pidgin incomprehensible to parents
a decree was issued to build houses on sand only
and they build them higher and higher you can't crane your neck
high enough the roofs of the buildings are lost in the clouds
the elders were mobilized and serve in heavenly squadrons
All will be swell life a bowl of cherries as long as our luck
holds out and the occupants are not cast down into Hades
while the military hardware isn't rusting on dumping grounds
until the adolescents with ear and nose piercings don't die out
the motherland herself is to blame raising them without scruples
and now a spinster she stands off by herself alone till the end of days
the loaf of bread turned to stone on it the empty salt shaker

Translated by Alex Cigale

Что ж ты сидишь, как в гостях,
а ноги не вытер?
Всякий город стоит на костях,
а не только Питер.

Нужно строить дома на камне,
а не на болоте.
Все так, но пока мне
нет радости в этой работе.

Жизнь моя – на весах,
и нет счета потерям.
Лучше мне быть в лесах
большим неуклюжим зверем.

Я бы валежник ломал,
пробираясь к себе в берлогу,
морду вверх поднимал
и рычал бы Господу Богу.

WHY SIT LIKE A GUEST BUT NOT WIPE YOUR FEET

Why sit like a guest
but not wipe your feet?
Every town's built on bones,
not just St. Pete.

One should build homes on stone,
not on a bog.
True enough, but for now
the work is a slog.

My life's on the scales—
the losses won't cease.
Let me dwell in the woods—
a big clumsy beast.

I'd crawl back to my lair
across the dry forest floor,
raise my snout in the air
and roar up at the Lord.

Translated by Boris Dralyuk

Вони написали в історії хвороби:
«Ніякого голодування не було
Була стійка маячня Ганни Михайленко,
Вчительки української літератури».
Сім років була вона у спеціальній Психіатричній лікарні.
То була гібридна лікарня –
 Суміш дурдома й в'язниці.
Тоді гібридна лікарня. Зараз гібридна війна.
Сім років – біблійний термін.
Сім років служив Яків Лавану За Рахіль,
бо він любив її. Сім років.
«Плаче Рахіль за дітьми своїми
Й не може утішитись,
Бо їх нема».

THEY PRINTED IN THE MEDICAL HISTORY

They printed in the medical history:
"There was no Holodomor.
It was the stable delusion of Anna Mikhailenko,
a teacher of Ukrainian literature."
For seven years she was in a Special Psychiatric Hospital.
It was a hybrid hospital—
a madhouse and a prison.
It was a time of hybrid hospitals. Now is time of a hybrid war.
Seven years is a biblical phrase.
"And Jacob served Laban seven years for Rachel.
Because he loved her."
Seven. Seven years.
"Rachel calls for her children.
She can't calm herself,
Because they don't exist."

Translated by Katie Farris and Ilya Kaminsky

БЕССАРАБИЯ, ГАЛИЦИЯ, 1913 - 1939
ИЗРЕЧЕНИЯ

1

Ребе Ицхак Леви сказал:
«Есть нечто сходное у людей и деревьев –
наши корни в земле».

2

Ребе Шрага Мендлович сказал:
«Это сужденье содержит неточность,
ибо корни деревьев целы
и наполнены влагой,
даже если земля суха,
а наши корни
разрозненны и иссохли».

3

Ребе Ицхак Штайнмахер сказал:
«Эта разница несущественна,
ибо мертвые или живые,
но наши корни – питают».

4

Ребе Шломо бен Иегуда сказал:
«Мы не властны судить о том,
живы ли наши корни,
ибо у нас есть Помощник,
обещавший нам воскресение
и верный обетованию».

5

Ребе Ицхак Штайнмахер сказал:
«Вот вы рассуждаете,
а мне не дает покоя
образ родословного древа.
Мы рисуем ствол возвышающимся,

BESSARABIA, GALICIA, 1913 - 1939
PRONOUNCEMENTS

1

And rabbi Yitzchak Levi said:
"People and trees share this—
roots in the earth."

2

And rabbi Shraga Mendlowitz said:
"This observation is inexact
for the roots of trees are whole and quenched, even as the earth is dry,
while our roots—
our roots
are withered and torn."

3

And rabbi Yitzchak Steinmacher said:
"This difference is nonessential
for, whether living or dead: all roots still nurture."

4

And rabbi Shlomo ben Yehuda said:
"It's not up to us to say whether our roots are alive:
for we have a Helper,
who promised us eternal life—
and is true to his promise."

5

And rabbi Yitzchak Steinmacher said:
"Listening to you
I cannot help but think of a genealogical tree. We picture its trunk
    ascending,
its branches—
mighty and wide; the name of our ancestor is a fruit
that's ripe.
In truth: a genealogical tree

ветви — мощными и широкими;
имя предка подобно плоду,
созревшему и совершенному.
Но на деле родословное древо
постепенно погружается в землю.
Истинно, у него не только корни в земле,
но и ствол, и мощные ветви,
а мы — немудрые листья,
освещенные солнцем Торы,
о чем мы толкуем здесь?»

6

Ребе Шрага Мендлович сказал:
«Увы!
Как печально измыслить дерево,
приращиваемое смертью,
углубляющееся в землю.
Я думаю, в этом присутствует
тонкое заблуждение:
ибо наши корни в Земле,
а эта земля — не Земля,
но пустыня скитаний. —
И, возвышая голос,
ребе Шрага продолжил:
— Истинно вам говорю:
если кто-то когда-то дерзнет
просеивать сквозь тончайшее сито
песок Синайской пустыни,
чтобы найти останки
тех, кто шел из Египта, —
не обретет ничего,
ибо наши корни — в Земле,
а эта земля — не Земля».

7

И сказали все четверо:
«Благословенно ты, древо,

descends
into the earth. Verily, not only its roots are in the earth
but so are its trunk
and branches.
As for us: we are the ignorant leaves
under the sun of Torah,
ignorant,
what do we say to each other?"

6
And rabbi Shraga Mendlowitz said:
"Ah!
It grieves me to think of a tree
that grows into its death,
that descends into the earth.
There might be a subtle deception
in this image:
for our roots are in the Earth,
while this earth is not the Earth,
but a desert of wandering."
And raising his voice,
rabbi Shraga went on:
"Verily I say unto Thou:
if somebody dares
to sift in the finest of sieves through the sand of Sinai
in order to find the remains
of those traveling from Egypt, he'd find nothing,
for our roots are in the Earth,
and this earth—is not the Earth."

7
And all four of them said:
"Blessed be the tree growing into the Earth,
submerged into the Earth.
Blessed be You, Who
has this tree shaking
in awe,

растущее в Землю
и погруженное в Землю.
Благословен Ты, Который
заставляешь его сотрясаться
в благоговейном страхе,
содрогаться целиком,
от тончайшей ветки до корня.
Ибо вот содрогание это,
вернее, сама способность
ужасаться и содрогаться
от страха или от боли,
есть признак присутствия жизни».

•

Много позже, в семидесятых,
после шестидневной войны,
археологи предприняли раскопки
в Синайской пустыне
в поисках того, что они называют
материальными остатками сорокалетнего
странствия евреев в пустыне.

•

Они не нашли ничего.

shuddering end to end, from its thinnest twig to its root.
For this shudder,
for the chance
to know terror and to shudder from fear and pain,
is exactly
the proof of life."

•

Much later, in the 70s,
after the Six-Day War,
archaeologists attempted an excavation
in the Sinai desert
in search of what they call
material evidence of forty-years of wandering
in the desert.

•

And they found? Nothing.

Translated by Valzhyna Mort

взрывы норма жизни с ними сживаясь ты
перестаешь замечать человек что тебе кранты
ходят по парку парою подрывник и сапер
шепчут друг другу на ухо интересно о чем разговор

понятно о смысле действий где лопата там и подкоп,
где заговор там и подвох, где подлость там и подлог
у бабушки на огороде вырос честный укроп
где тетушка там бузина где Бог там и порог

понятно о смысле смерти негаданной как обвал
понятно о водке чтоб смертный об утратах не горевал
где ума палата там в палате строгий надзор
где усики черным квадратом там волосы на пробор

ходят парою по аллее сапер и друг подрывник
ангел губитель с облака с нежностью смотрит на них
мы подневольные птицы пора брат давно пора
сияет черное солнце осколочная дыра

EXPLOSIONS ARE THE NEW NORMAL

explosions norm of life coming to terms with them you
stop noticing man it be your end
the sapper and demolition man arm-in-arm in the park
whisper in each other's ear what are they saying

get the gist of the action shovel means undermine
conspiracy means undermine, underhanded means overkill
granny grew plain dill* under the rain that fell mainly
elderly lady means elderberry, God means year

you get the gist of death out of the blue avalanche
gist of vodka for mortals to handle loss
mind means undermined means over and out
black square of a mustache means till death do we part

sapper and demolition pal arm-in-arm in the alley
terminating angel beholds them holds them with love
we are unfreebirds good night sweet prints turning read
shines the black sun the no one's rose of a shell shard

Translated by Vladislav Davidzon and Eugene Ostashevsky

Translator's Note: *Ukrop* is a slang neologism that literally means "dill" in Russian. It is a derogatory term for Ukrainians with roots in the fighting of the Donbas, which was later appropriated by the Ukrainians and became something Ukrainians refer to themselves as. It now adorns patriotic T-shirts with a picture of dill and word *ukrop*.

НАКАЗАНИЕ

Все звери когда-то были людьми, но потом
все согрешили – сами тому виной.
И Бог наслал на всех людей всемирный потоп,
и всех бывших людей по паре вывез в ковчеге Ной.
Каждый из них был порочен, блудлив и лжив.
Ослушанье и грех никогда не приводят к добру.
Все они провинились и, согрешив,
на глаза попались Господу и святому Петру.
И их превратили – каждого за свой грех –
кого в вола – пахали на нем, кого в коня – били плетьми.
А тех людей, кто провинился более всех,
Бог в наказание так и оставил людьми.

PUNISHMENT

All animals were once human, but then
they sinned—
and God flooded our Earth
and Noah smuggled all those former humans in pairs.
Each of them
was wicked, deceitful. And so God
and St. Peter turned each of them
into an ox, to plow the field, into
a horse to be whipped. But those
who were most deceitful, God
left in shape of human beings, as a punishment.

Translated by Katie Farris and Ilya Kaminsky

на фоне молчания муз слышнее гром канонады
на фоне рыдания вдов слышнее смех клоунады
кто богат тот и рад а мы бедны и не рады
на фоне синего неба страшней облаков громады
что в реке не потонет то зарастет травою
на фоне блеянья стад просторнее волчьему вою
где базар там и вор а там и блатной разговор
а там и перо под ребро или выстрел у упор
на фоне добра есть где разгуляться злу
в огне всегда найдется чему превратиться в золу
нож в кармане чужом и сам ты ходишь с ножом
на фоне лжи не заметно что сами мы тоже лжем

AGAINST THE BACKDROP OF SILENT MUSES

against the backdrop of silent muses heavy gunfire thunders louder
against the background of grieving windows the clowns laugh louder
the rich are happy but we're poor and unhappy
against the blue skied background the crowds of clouds are terrifying
what won't drown in a river will overgrow with grass
against the backdrop of bleating flocks there's more room
    for the howling wolves
where there's a market there's a thief and conniving
and then there's a shank in your ribcage or gunshots at point blank
against the backdrop of the good there's room for evil
in the fire there's always something that could turn to ash
a knife in someone's pocket and a knife in your pocket
against the background of lies it's not apparent that we're also liars

Translated by Javier Zamora with Oksana Maksymchuk

взрывы норма жизни с ними сживаясь ты
перестаешь замечать человек что тебе кранты
ходят по парку парою подрывник и сапер
шепчут друг другу на ухо интересно о чем разговор

понятно о смысле действий где лопата там и подкоп,
где заговор там и подвох, где подлость там и подлог
у бабушки на огороде вырос честный укроп
где тетушка там бузина где Бог там и порог

понятно о смысле смерти негаданной как обвал
понятно о водке чтоб смертный об утратах не горевал
где ума палата там в палате строгий надзор
где усики черным квадратом там волосы на пробор

ходят парою по аллее сапер и друг подрывник
ангел губитель с облака с нежностью смотрит на них
мы подневольные птицы пора брат давно пора
сияет черное солнце осколочная дыра

EXPLOSIONS ARE THE NEW NORMAL

explosions are the new normal, you grow used to them
stop noticing that you, with your ordinary ways, are a goner
a trigger man and a sapper wander around the park
whispering like a couple—I wish I could eavesdrop
surely, it goes this way: where there's a shovel, there's a tunnel
where there's a conspiracy, there's a catch
where there's God, there's a threshold
stalky Ukrainians—where granny tends to a garden patch
surely it's about the meaning of death, sudden as a mudslide
surely it's about the vodka: to relieve mortal anguish
once you've shown you have any brain, they'll brain you hard
    into submission
hair impeccably parted—where you spot a geometrically neat moustache
a trigger man and a sapper wander around like a couple
as the angel of destruction observes them tenderly from the cloud
we're captive birds dear brother that's it that's all
black sun of melancholy shines like a shrapnel hole

Translated by Polina Barskova and Ostap Kin

я читаю с акцентом даже тогда
когда читаю книгу и рта открыть не умею
речь гудит как на ветру провода
ничего не исправишь пора бросить эту затею
язык за зубами губа прижата к губе
фонетика и морфология лингвистика вот науки
они меня одолели в долгой упорной борьбе
и водят вокруг хороводы взявшись за руки
я даже мыслю с акцентом как бы сказал декарт
я существую с акцентом жизнь подобно училке
идет мимо дней моих как между рядами парт
и что-то знакомое чудится в злобной ее ухмылке

I READ WITH AN ACCENT

I read with an accent and I can't open I
can't open my mouth speech snaps like a wire
in the wind, what can't be fixed? Tongue
behind teeth, lip pressed to lip, phonetics
and linguistics drown me in me;
morphology whips dances around my body holding hands
with semantics I even think with an accent, Descartes
might say I breathe with an accent, life a teacher
lingers between my days like rows
of desks, how like my own is her wicked grin.

Translated by Katie Farris and Ilya Kaminsky

После победы – эпоха казней послевоенных.
Скоротечные заседания и решения трибуналов.
Необходимо уменьшить поголовье военнопленных.
Не кормить же в тюрьме побежденных вражеских генералов!

Тем более, что у каждого руки в крови по локоть.
И сохранились приказы, что они отдавали солдатам.
Ибо страсть к убийству – та же сексуальная похоть.
Начнешь и не остановишься, и хотелось бы – да куда там!

И теперь вверх по лесенкам, руки связаны за спиною,
в сопровождении пасторов, или ксендзов – если католик,
и – мешок на голову, петлю на шею, умирай со своею виною,
через семьдесят лет в ютубе выложат ролик.

Пять минут и живой человек теперь уже мертвое тело.
Еще пять минут и гроб уже заколочен.
Жалеть военных преступников – это последнее дело.
Была бы веревка прочна или выстрел точен.

Все дело теперь в палаче и его сноровке.
Лишение жизни дешевле, чем лишенье свободы.
И вся справедливость мира в пуле или веревке.
А другой справедливости нет в послевоенные годы.

WHEN VICTORY IS OURS—
POSTWAR EXECUTIONS START

When victory is ours—the postwar executions start.
The hasty meetings, the tribunals passing sentence.
We need to thin the ranks of all these prisoners of war.
Why should we feed the generals we've vanquished?

They've got as much blood on their hands as all the rest.
We have the orders that they gave their men.
The urge to murder is a form of sexual lust.
You just can't stop—you want to, but you can't.

And so it's up the ladder, hands behind their backs,
with pastors—priests, if they should happen to be Catholics—
bags on their heads, nooses around their necks.
Die, scum. In seven decades, you'll get YouTube clicks.

Five minutes—and a man is a dead body.
Another five—the coffin is nailed shut.
War criminals deserve no hint of pity.
A strong rope is enough, or a sure shot.

The executioner—his skill—is our great hope.
Prison's expensive—killing simply costs less.
The only justice is the bullet and the rope.
The postwar era knows no other justice.

Translated by Boris Dralyuk

Земля отражается дважды – в море и в небесах.
Три слоя реальности, которую не разделить.
Попасть в этот мир означает попасть впросак.
Все равно могилу копать или постель стелить.

Это ловушка – из нее не уйти живым.
Это лепешка пресного теста – пожалте в печь.
Ветер гонит обрывки мыслей по мостовым.
Не прощайся с жизнью, скажи ей – до новых встреч!

THE EARTH IS REFLECTED TWICE

The earth is reflected twice: in the sea and the sky.
Three layers of reality—that can't be split.
As soon as you land in this world you're hung out to dry.
Digging a grave is the same as making a bed.

This whole thing is a trap: no way out but to die.
This whole thing is a flop: a flapjack, flimsy and thin.
In the wind scraps of thoughts fall to the pavement and fly.
No final farewells—tell life: we'll meet again.

Translated by Boris Dralyuk

по городу носят взрывчатку в пластиковых пакетах
хозяйственных сумках и маленьких чемоданах
топчут асфальт и брусчатку мы узнаем об их секретах
после взрывов и это просто уточнение данных

сколько окон выбито сколько балконов упало
есть ли убитые или все живы здоровы
только напуганы тем что мирной жизни не стало
случилась война а законы войны суровы

или их просто нет и взрывы вошли в привычку
не встаем из-за столика только вздрогнем и лица мрачнее
враг выбирает оружие как вор подбирает отмычку
а дверь открыта и так говоря точнее

PEOPLE CARRY EXPLOSIVES AROUND THE CITY

people carry explosives around the city
in plastic shopping bags and little suitcases
they trample the cobblestone we learn their secrets
only the day after and even then it's just checking the facts

how many windows shattered how many collapsed balconies
did anyone die or is everyone alive and kicking
only frightened that there is no more peaceful life perhaps
war happened and the laws of war are a cruel thing

or perhaps there are no more laws and explosions are now the norm
we don't get up from the table just shiver and shed some hope
an enemy chooses weapons as a thief finds the pick for a door
when in fact the door was already open

Translated by Olga Livshin and Andrew Janco

утренний дождь сильнее чем тусклый утренний свет
бумажный кораблик плывет раньше он был портрет
правителя, но его сложили особым образом вот
он теперь бумажный кораблик, не знает куда плывет

какое странное лето ни солнышка ни тепла
дождь зарядил с утра жизнь была да сплыла
плывут по течению мысли и фильтры от сигарет
плывет бумажный кораблик раньше он был портрет

THIS MORNING'S RAIN OVERPOWERS
THE DIM MORNING LIGHT

this morning's rain overpowers the dim morning light
a paper boat floats on the current it was at one point
the head-of-state's portrait but folded just right
it's a boat that knows not where it floats

a peculiar summer no sunlight no warmth
been pouring all day and life wouldn't stay
thoughts and cigarette filters also drift off
a boat once a portrait is floating away

Translated by Boris Dralyuk

запиши меня в книгу жизни запиши
огненным пером из крыла керуба
в огромную книгу взятую в переплет
из кедровых досок обтянутых кожей
с коваными застежками из красной меди
запиши меня в книгу жизни запиши
в книгу тяжелую как сама жизнь
которую не поднять не понять
на страницу которую не перевернуть
всю в пометках как школьный журнал
переведен в следующий класс
в следующий год
в следующий раз
успеваемость посещаемость поведение
никуда не годилось вряд ли исправится
нужно вызвать родителей
прародителей
до седьмого-восьмого колена
запиши меня в книгу страницы
в каплях воска крови чернил спермы
без чего не бывает жизни
черный ангел летит с шофаром
летит и трубит в полете
мне не страшно честное слово
запиши меня в книгу жизни
в кожаном переплете

WRITE ME INTO THE BOOK OF LIFE

write me into the book of life write me
with a burning feather plucked from a cherub's wing
into a huge book bound out of cedar planks
wrapped in leather wrought by red copper clasps
write me into a book of life write me
into a book heavy as life itself
which we can't lift can't understand
not even a page can be turned
all marked up like a school record book
transfer him to another class
another year
another time
attendance academic progress conduct
good for nothing improvement improbable
call his parents up
ancestors
seven/eight generations back

write me into the pages
in drops of wax blood ink cum
without which there is no life

a dark angel flies with a shofar
playing his trumpet in flight
I'm not afraid I give you my word
write me into the book of life
bound in leather

Translated by Javier Zamora with Oksana Maksymchuk

AUTHORS' NOTE

We dedicate this book to the memory of Alexander Roitburd—our friend, an artist, a man of great energy and love of life. Since the days of the Maidan Revolution and the subsequent war, we stood together firmly with Ukraine, for its democratic future. And we believe that these days, and he, are with us.

EDITORS' NOTE

We are grateful to Boris and Lyudmyla Khersonsky for reading these translations and for their poems and their friendship. Our gratitude also to all the translators for their work, and to Christine Holbert and Grace Mahoney for guiding this project. Thank you.

EDITORS

Katie Farris is the author of *Boysgirls* (Tupelo Press), *A Net to Catch My Body in Its Weaving* (Beloit PJ) and *Standing in the Forest of Being Alive* (Alice James, 2023). Farris co-edited *Gossip and Metaphysics: Russian Modernist Poets* (Tupelo Press). She teaches at Georgia Tech.

Ilya Kaminsky is the author of *Dancing in Odessa* (Tupelo Press) and *Deaf Republic* (Graywolf Press). He co-translated *Dark Elderberry Branch: Poems of Marina Tsvetaeva* (Alice James) and co-edited *Ecco Anthology of International Poetry* (Harper Collins). He teaches at Georgia Tech.

TRANSLATORS

Polina Barskova's books in English translation include *This Lamentable City* (Tupelo Press), *The Zoo in Winter* (Melville House), *Relocations* (Zephyr Press) and *Air Raid* (Ugly Duckling). She teaches at UC Berkeley.

Alex Cigale's translations include Daniil Kharms' *Russian Absurd: Selected Writing* which is available from Northwestern University Press's World Classics Series. Cigale teaches at CYNY-Queens College.

Vladislav Davidzon is the author of *From Odessa With Love: Political and Literary Essays from Post-Soviet Ukraine* (Academica Press). His work has appeared in *Tablet* magazine and *The Critic*. He is the Editor-in-Chief of *Odessa Review*.

Boris Dralyuk translated Isaac Babel's *Red Calvary* and *Odessa Stories* (both from Pushkin Press) and Mikhail Zoshchenko's *Sentimental Tales* (Columbia). He is also the author of a collection of poetry, *My Hollywood and Other Poems* (Paul Dry Books, 2022).

Katie Farris is the editor of this book.

Andrew Janco's translations of poetry appear in *Words for War: New Poems from Ukraine* (Academic Studies Press), and his scholarship appears in *Slavic Review*. He is a librarian at Haverford College.

Ilya Kaminsky is the editor of this book.

Ostap Kin is the editor of *New York Elegies: Ukrainian Poems on the City* (Academic Studies Press) and, with Vitaly Chernetsky, translator of *Songs for a Dead Rooster* (Lost Horse Press) by Yuri Andrukhovych.

Olga Livshin is the author of *A Life Replaced: Poems with Translations from Anna Akhmatova and Vladimir Gandelsman* (Poets and Traitors Press). Her works appears in journals such as *The Kenyon Review* and *The Los Angeles Review of Books*.

Grace Mahoney is the translator of Iryna Starovoyt's *A Field of Foundlings* (Lost Horse Press). Mahoney is also the Series Editor of the Lost Horse Press Contemporary Ukrainian Poetry Series.

Valzhyna Mort books include *Factory of Tears, Collected Body* (both from Copper Canyon Press), and *Music for the Dead and Resurrected* (FSG). She has translated Polina Barskova's *Air Raid* (Ugly Duckling). Mort teaches at Cornell University.

Eugene Ostashevsky is the author of the poetry collections *The Life and Opinions of DJ Spinoza* and *Iterature* (both published by Ugly Duckling Press), and *The Pirate Who Does Not Know the Value of Pi* (NYRB). He is the translator of Alexander Vvedensky.

Diane Seuss's most recent collection is *frank: sonnets* (Graywolf Press, 2021). She was a 2020 Guggenheim Fellow, and she received the John Updike Award from the American Academy of Arts and Letters in 2021.

Katherine E. Young's books include *Day of the Border Guards* (The University of Arkansas Press) and *Woman Drinking Absinthe* (Alan Squire Publishing). She has translated several books including Anna Starobinets' *Look at Him* (Slavica Publishers).

Javier Zamora was born in El Salvador and migrated to the US when he was nine. He is the author of *Unaccompanied* (Copper Canyon Press, 2017) and *Solito: A Memoir* (Hogarth, 2022).